# Harriet Tubman

### by Wil Mara

### Content Consultant

Nanci R. Vargus, Ed.D.
Professor Emeritus, University of Indianapolis

### Reading Consultant

Jeanne Clidas, Ph.D.

**Children's Press®**
An Imprint of Scholastic Inc.
New York Toronto London Auckland Sydney
Mexico City New Delhi Hong Kong
Danbury, Connecticut

Cataloging-in-Publication Data is available from the Library of Congress

ISBN 978-0-531-24737-2 (lib. bdg.)
ISBN 978-0-531-24703-7 (pbk.)

Produced by Spooky Cheetah Press
Poem by Jodie Shepherd

Printed in China 62

SCHOLASTIC, CHILDREN'S PRESS, ROOKIE BIOGRAPHIES®, and associated logos are trademarks and/or registered trademarks of Scholastic Inc.

1 2 3 4 5 6 7 8 9 10 R 22 21 20 19 18 17 16 15 14 13

Photographs © 2013: Alamy Images/Anthony Pleva: 3 top right; AP Images: cover (Manuel Balce Ceneta), 15, 27, 31 center top (North Wind Picture Archives), 12 (Wilton Historical Society, Douglas Healey); Getty Images: 24, 31 bottom (Buyenlarge), 3 bottom (Fotosearch), 7 (Mondadori); Janice N. Huse/http:// JaniceHuse.com: 16, 19, 31 top; Library of Congress: 4, 30 left (H.B. Lindsley), 11 (James F. Gibson); Shutterstock, Inc./igor gratzer: 3 top left, 30 right; Smith College/William Cheney/Sophia Smith Collection: 23; Superstock, Inc./Ambient Images Inc.: 28; The Granger Collection: 20, 31 center bottom.

Maps by XNR Productions, Inc.

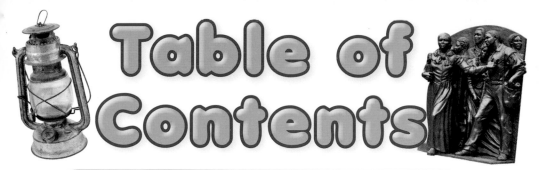

# Table of Contents

# Meet Harriet Tubman

Harriet Tubman was very brave. She spent her life fighting slavery. A slave is someone who is owned by another person.

This photo of Harriet was taken when she was about 40 or 50 years old.

A long time ago, there was slavery in the United States. Most slaves, like Harriet, were African Americans. Many worked on large farms. They did not get paid to work. They had very hard lives.

Many slaves worked all day in the hot sun. Even children had to work.

7

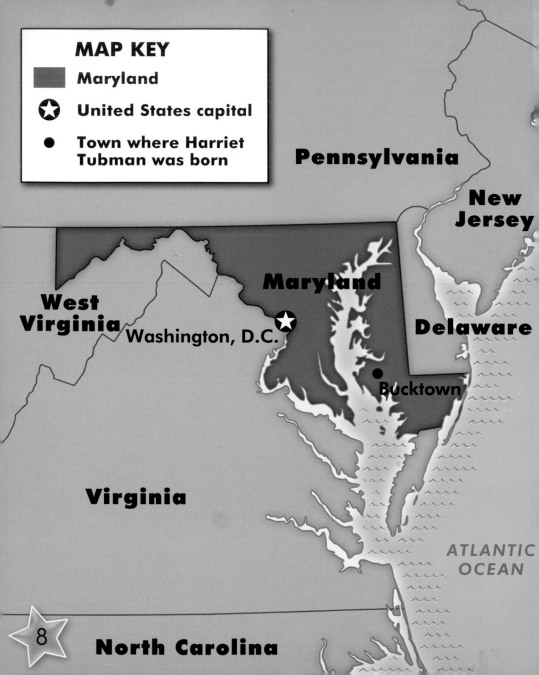

MAP KEY

Maryland

★ United States capital

● Town where Harriet Tubman was born

Pennsylvania

New Jersey

West Virginia

Washington, D.C.

Maryland

Delaware

Bucktown

Virginia

ATLANTIC OCEAN

North Carolina

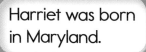

Harriet was born in Maryland.

Harriet Tubman was born in Maryland around 1820. She was a slave. Most slaves were not allowed to play or go to school.

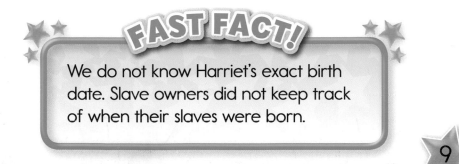

FAST FACT!

We do not know Harriet's exact birth date. Slave owners did not keep track of when their slaves were born.

The people who owned Harriet treated her badly. They beat her many times. Like all slaves, Harriet had to do whatever her owners told her to do.

If a slave woman had children, they were slaves, too.

11

# Escape!

Harriet ran away in 1849. She **escaped** with the help of the Underground Railroad. It was not a real railroad. It was a group of people who helped slaves escape to states where there was no slavery.

Homes with hidden tunnels were used by the Underground Railroad to help slaves escape.

Harriet escaped to Pennsylvania. The state of Pennsylvania was a "free" state. That means there was no slavery there.

Slaves who tried to escape faced great danger. Their owners always tried to catch them.

15

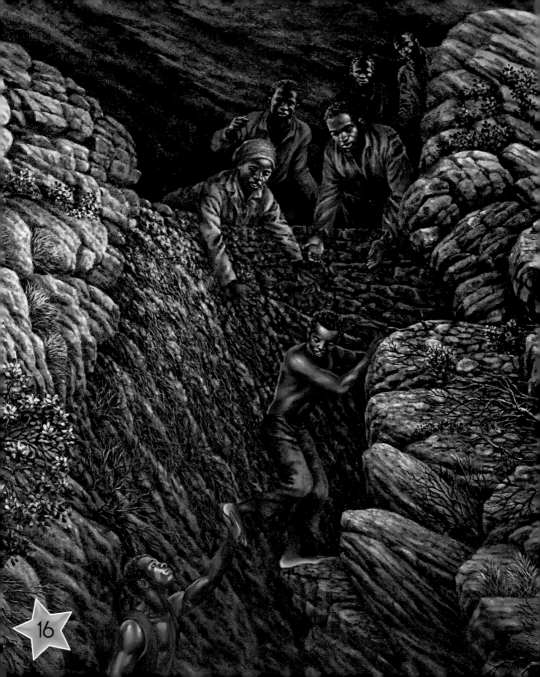

# A Dangerous Life

Harriet wanted to help other slaves run away. She became part of the Underground Railroad. It was very **dangerous** work.

Harriet risked her life many times to help slaves escape.

Harriet moved the runaway slaves in the middle of the night. She led them from one stop on the Underground Railroad to the next.

Harriet never failed to bring her followers to safety.

20

Many people wanted to stop Harriet. They said they would give a lot of money to whoever caught her.

Harriet was willing to fight to make people free.

Harriet did not worry about getting caught. She helped more than 300 slaves leave their owners.

**FAST FACT!**

Harriet managed to free both of her parents and some of her eight brothers and sisters.

Harriet (far left) poses with some of the people she helped.

24

Many battles were fought
during the Civil War.

# Free at Last!

A **war** began in the United States
in 1861. This was the Civil War. Slave
states fought against free states.
Harriet helped the free states.

**FAST FACT!**

During the Civil War, Harriet
worked as a nurse and a **spy**.

The Civil War ended in 1865. The free states won. Slavery was no longer allowed. All slaves were set free. Harriet spent the rest of her life helping people who had been slaves.

Ex-slaves hurried to leave their old lives behind. Many traveled to states in the North.

## Timeline of Harriet Tubman's Life

**1820**
born a slave
in Maryland

**1849**
runs away to
Pennsylvania

**1850**
begins working on the
Underground Railroad

Harriet turned her home in New York into a place for ex-slaves to live.

Harriet died in 1913. She will always be remembered for the great risks she faced so that others could be free.

**1861**
is a nurse and a spy during the Civil War

**1913**
dies on March 10

**1859**
buys a home in New York that she uses to help hide runaway slaves

**1903**
turns her house over to poor black families

# A Poem About Harriet Tubman

*"Come with me," says Harriet,*
*"and hop aboard my freedom train.*
*And when the ride is finally done,*
*you'll never be a slave again."*

## You Can Help Others

- You can do chores for an older person in your neighborhood or give food and clothes to a shelter for homeless people.

- Give your time to help a charity you believe in.

# Glossary

**dangerous** (DAYN-jur-us): something that is not safe

**escaped** (ess-KAPED): ran away from something bad

**spy** (spye): someone who works for one country to find out secret information about another

**war** (wor): a fight between two groups of people

31

# Index

# Facts for Now

Visit this Scholastic Web site for more information on Harriet Tubman:
**www.factsfornow.scholastic.com**
Enter the keywords **Harriet Tubman**

# About the Author

Wil Mara is the award-winning author of more than 140 books, many of which are educational titles for children.